First Facts®

Transportation Zone

Subways

in Action

by Allison Lassieur

CAPSTONE PRESS
a capstone imprint

First Facts is published by Capstone Press,
1710 Roe Crest Drive, North Mankato, Minnesota 56003.
www.capstonepub.com

Books published by Capstone Press are manufactured with paper
containing at least 10 percent post-consumer waste.

Library of Congress Cataloging-in-Publication Data
Lassieur, Allison.
 Subways in action / by Allison Lassieur.
      p. cm.—(First facts. Transportation zone)
 Includes bibliographical references and index.
 Summary: "Discusses the history, function, and workings of subways"—Provided by
publisher.
 ISBN 978-1-4296-7690-8 (library binding)
 ISBN 978-1-4296-7967-1 (paperback)
 1. Subways—Juvenile literature. I. Title.
 TF845.L276 2012
 625.4′2—dc23   2011021522

Editorial Credits
Christine Peterson and Rebecca Glaser, editors; Sarah Bennett and Lori Bye, designers;
    Eric Gohl, media researcher; Kathy McColley, production specialist

Image Credits
Capstone Studio/Karon Dubke, 22
Dreamstime/Sean Pavone, 19
Getty Images/Bloomberg/Bernardo De Niz, 9
iStockphoto/Denis Tangney Jr., 11; Duncan Walker, 17; Hulton Archive, 15
    (top); Robert Van Beets, 1
Library of Congress, 12; 15 (bottom)
Shutterstock/Rafael Ramirez Lee, cover; Rudy Balasko, 21; ssguy, 4;
    Tupungato, 7; Yusef El-Mansouri, 6

Printed in the United States of America in North Mankato, Minnesota.

042015   008802NYC

Table of Contents

The Subway

With a whoosh and
a roar, subways speed
through dark tunnels. This
system of underground
trains is a fast way to
transport people. Subways
carry people to different
parts of a city. In large
cities, subways keep streets
from becoming clogged
with traffic.

Traveling by Subway

Passengers board subway trains at stations. Stations are wide parts of a tunnel. Stations have platforms where people get on and off the trains.

To Union Station

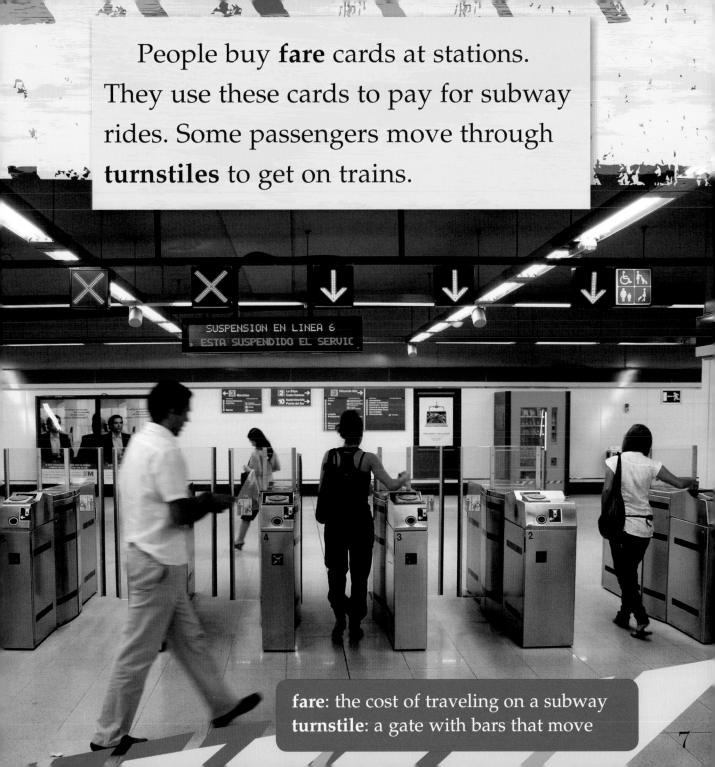

People buy **fare** cards at stations. They use these cards to pay for subway rides. Some passengers move through **turnstiles** to get on trains.

fare: the cost of traveling on a subway
turnstile: a gate with bars that move

7

Parts of a Subway

Most subways have similar parts. An operator drives the subway from the front car. Drivers follow signs and approach signals to drive trains safely. Subway cars have sliding doors, large windows, and many seats. Computers control some modern subway trains. Operators **monitor** these trains from a control room.

monitor: to watch closely

How a Subway Works

A subway train travels on two rails. The train's wheels roll on the rails. Electricity flows through a third rail beside the main rails. The electricity powers small motors under each subway car. The motors make the subway move.

main rail

third rail

wheel

carriage

Before Subways

People traveled in horse-drawn **carriages** or walked before the subway was invented. Travel from one part of a city to another took a long time. As cities grew larger, public transportation systems developed. In some cities, people rode in cable cars or electric streetcars.

carriage: a vehicle with wheels that is usually pulled by horses

The First Subway

City planner Charles Pearson had an idea for an underground train system in London, England. Workers dug **trenches**. They built sides and a roof on the trenches to form a tunnel. London's first subway opened in 1863.

In 1870 Alfred Beach built America's first subway in New York City. Big fans blew air into the tunnel to push the subway train. New York's underground subway opened in 1904.

trench: a long, narrow ditch in the ground

London subway, 1863

early subway in New York City

Early Subway Trains

Steam powered early subway trains. Subway workers burned coal to heat water. The heated water made steam. Steam-powered trains produced dark smoke from the coal fires. Smoke filled the subway tunnels and made everything dirty.

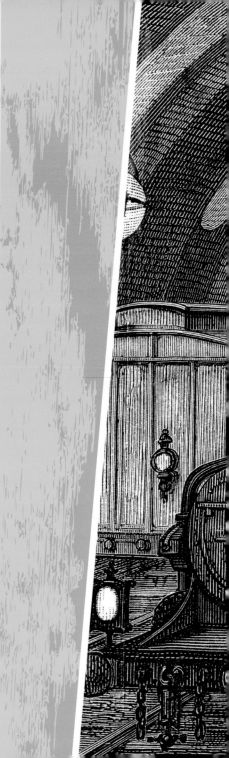

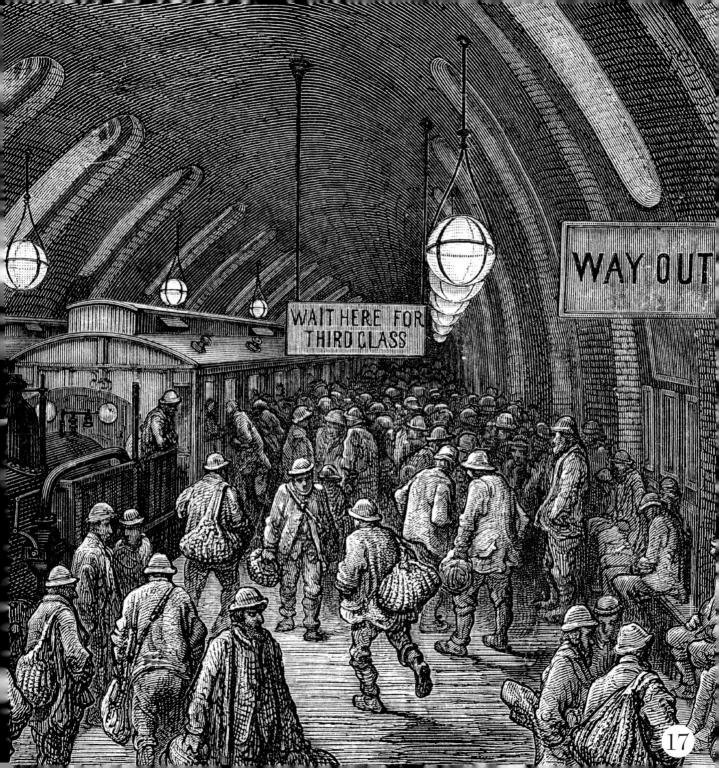

Subways around the World

Subways are an **efficient** form of transportation around the world. The world's longest subway is in China. The Shanghai Metro covers 270 miles (435 kilometers). It averages 5.2 million riders a day. About 3 billion people ride subways each year in Tokyo, Japan. Subways will serve the world's cities for years to come.

efficient: not wasteful of time or energy

Subway Facts

- In New York City, about 1.6 billion people ride the subway each year.

- Subway trains in Tokyo are very crowded. During busy times, more than 300 people may ride in one car.

- Subway tunnels in San Francisco, California, and Mexico City, Mexico, are built to hold up during earthquakes.

- Subway trains called Els sometimes travel on or above the ground.

- London's subway system is called the Underground. But passengers also call it the "Tube."

- Some subway trains do not run on rails. They have rubber tires that run in narrow trenches.

El train

Hands On: Build a Model Subway Tunnel

Many subway tunnels are built using the cut-and-cover method. Workers cut a trench through an area. They then cover it with a roof. Build your own cut-and-cover tunnel.

What You Need

a small shovel
sandy area, such as a sandbox

a shoebox with lid
scissors

What You Do

1. Dig a trench in the sandy area. Make the trench deep enough to put the shoebox inside. Make the trench longer than the shoebox.
2. Cut a hole in each end of the shoebox. Leave 1 inch (2.5 centimeters) on each side and 2 inches (5 cm) at the top.
3. Put the shoebox in the trench.
4. Put the lid on the shoebox.
5. Fill any spaces between the shoebox and the trench sides with sand. Cover the lid with sand.

The walls and lid of the shoebox are stronger than the sand. They hold up the tunnel roof. In a real subway tunnel, columns also help hold up the roof.

Glossary

carriage (KA-rij)—a vehicle with wheels that usually is pulled by horses

efficient (uh-FISH-uhnt)—not wasteful of time or energy

fare (FAIR)—the cost of traveling on a subway

monitor (MON-uh-tur)—to watch closely

transport (transs-PORT)—to move or carry something or someone from one place to another

trench (TRENCH)—a long, narrow ditch in the ground

turnstile (TURN-stile)—a gate with bars that lets only one person through at a time

Read More

Peppas, Lynn. *Big Buses.* Vehicles on the Move. New York: Crabtree Pub., 2011.

Ryan, Phillip. *Subways.* All Aboard! New York: PowerKids Press, 2011.

Internet Sites

FactHound offers a safe, fun way to find Internet sites related to this book. All of the sites on FactHound have been researched by our staff.

Here's all you do:

Visit *www.facthound.com*

Type in this code: 9781429676908

 Check out projects, games and lots more at **www.capstonekids.com**

Index